Frogs

FROGS

Art, Legend, History

Patrizia Ribuoli and Marina Robbiani
Series editor: Giorgio Coppin

The Bulfinch Library of Collectibles

A Bulfinch Press Book
Little, Brown and Company
Boston · Toronto · London

First North American Edition
Second printing, 1992
English translation by John Gilbert
Series editor: Giorgio Coppin

ISBN 0–8212–1876–X
Library of Congress Catalog Card Number 91–55250
Library of Congress Cataloging-in-Publication information is available.

Bulfinch Press is an imprint and trademark of Little, Brown and Company (Inc.)
Published simultaneously in Canada by Little, Brown & Company (Canada) Limited

PRINTED IN ITALY

CONTENTS

Amphibian extraordinary

The frog – that unassuming creature of pond, lake and garden – is a remarkably successful animal that, in one form or another, has been around for some 150 million years. Hardly surprising, therefore, that it features so prominently throughout history, the world over, in legend and folklore, myth and magic, art and popular entertainment.

The frog, of course, is an amphibian. Life begins in fresh water and then runs its course principally on dry land, necessitating a complete change of body form and function. The adult is perfectly at ease in either element; and although he comes in a wide variety of shapes and sizes – there are, in fact, hundreds of species – the image generally conjured up is of a small green animal occasionally glimpsed squatting on a lily pad or hopping through the undergrowth. This is its normal manner of moving about on land, and perhaps its most characteristic and endearing feature.

This book does not set out to be a serious treatise on natural history, even though biology, physiology and the like are touched upon. It is an anthology rather than an encyclopedia. What it aims to do is to celebrate the frog in a wide diversity of guises and from many viewpoints. So it seems particularly appropriate to emulate that habit of our central subject and to skip from topic to topic more or less as fancy dictates – a dash of information here, a touch of fantasy there – and to invite the reader to do the same, in the hope that the end result will be instructive and, more importantly, entertaining.

We shall be looking at the frog, then, in a variety of contexts and associations. Suspended between history and myth, science and superstition, reality and dream, he emerges as the hero of adventure stories and fairy tales, the subject of laboratory research and the victim of culinary experiment, a symbol of psychoanalytical investigation and an inspiration for poets, playwrights, musicians and artists. He has become part and parcel of our everyday language, he fashions our idioms and proverbs, and his image has spanned the globe.

Our narrative contains an element of humour, and sometimes even a touch of the ridiculous: while bearing this in mind, the reader can then choose what to believe and what to take with a pinch of salt.

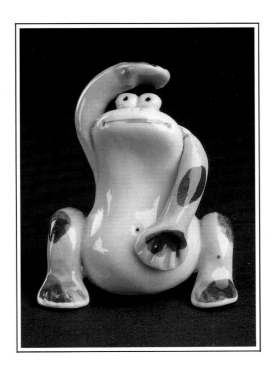

The ballerina frog (above) is amusing though certainly not as elegant as the Bolivian sculpture in black stone (opposite). On the following pages are a Chinese porcelain frog from the beginning of the century, and a soap dish with a frog decoration.

One thing has to be stressed at this early stage. Our central subject here is the frog, which along with its smaller and more elegant cousin, the tree frog, should not be confused with the toad. It may be opportune, therefore, to embark on a short diversion in order to discuss the principal features of both types of amphibian.

Frogs and toads are often to be found occupying the same habitats, whether in gardens or along the shores of pools and swamps. Although these animals are related, and thus display certain obvious similarities, they differ considerably in nature and habit. The true frogs belong to the family Ranidae, and the genus *Rana* is by far the largest and most widely distributed. The tailless tree frogs make up the family Hylidae

(the majority being species of the genus *Hyla*). They are, in fact, more closely related to the toads, likewise tailless, of the family Bufonidae (almost all belonging to genus *Bufo*).

One significant difference is that the frog is a completely harmless animal. The toad, on the other hand, if alarmed by an unwelcome or over-curious visitor, will instinctively go on the defensive, and in extreme cases may even launch a venomous attack. Beneath the toad's skin, two raised warty areas behind the eyes, the parotoid glands, secrete a strong dose of poison which, at the opportune moment, is squirted out. It may not be a decisive weapon but, if nothing else, it has the effect of deterring and confusing the enemy, giving the toad enough time to hop away to safety.

For someone unskilled in herpetology – the study of reptiles and amphibians – the two creatures may be distinguished at a glance by certain characteristic traits. The frog, for example, possesses small, sharp teeth, whereas the toad has none. The frog's skin is smooth and slippery, while that of the toad is rough and wrinkled. Furthermore, the toad has shorter legs than the frog and consequently cannot make such long jumps. There are substantial differences, too, in their respective

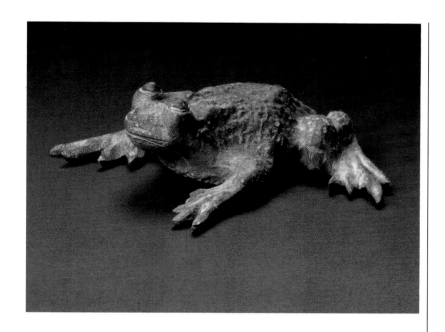

With its broad feet, ready to bound off, the impudent bronze frog above is a faithful reproduction of a statuette from the Roman period. Opposite: this frog from Bali, carved in turquoise, looks a good deal more cunning.

personalities. The toad is timid to the point of retirement, only daring to venture out at night when the concealment of shadows provides a feeling of security. Not that the frog is exactly a daredevil, for his shyness, too, is proverbial; but at least he plucks up the courage to go hunting by day, and if confronted by danger, he will put on a much braver show than his relation.

Although frogs and toads begin life in the same way, as tadpoles which breathe underwater through gills situated on either side of the neck, their life styles soon branch out in different directions. Preparation for the future may, in fact, be reflected in the habits of the breeding females. The mother toad, for instance, lays all her eggs close to one another, like pearls in a necklace, and these are attached together with a sticky substance. The female frog, for her part, lays her eggs in a single compact clump, rather like a dark soap bubble, which

is left to float on the pool surface. When the frog tadpole becomes an adult, it continues to live in and around the water, hunting small molluscs, insects and worms, but seldom venturing alone into the nearby grass. The toad, however, tends to wander more, settling in fields, woods and gardens.

Toads are long-lived (some individuals are as much as forty years old), sturdy and pain resistant. Among them are some strange species, with highly unusual habits, such as the Surinam toad of South America, *Pipa pipa*. The female lodges her eggs in pits along her back, covering them with a flap of skin until they are about to hatch: the tadpoles then force their way out and find continued protection on her back until they are fully grown.

Quite apart from biological distinctions, or perhaps arising from them, it has to be said that most people look on frogs as friendly, attractive creatures and regard toads as ugly and somehow threatening. Legend and folklore reflect these contrasting attitudes. Be that as it may, the frog is much the more popular of the two and far more frequently represented as ornaments, symbols and talismans. In Southeast Asia, for example, frogs fashioned of semi-precious stones are considered to be bringers of good fortune; in India, statuettes of frog-like images (often in gold) abound: and in Brazil, frog figures, again made of semi-precious stones, are used in magic rites as a guarantee of all kinds of good luck and plenty.

From Mexico – and indeed from most parts of Latin America – come plump, placid-looking frogs of terracotta, some of them beautifully hand painted, others elaborately carved into the form of flutes.

Just as much imagination and variety, if not taste, is to be found in Europe, where shop windows display fashionable toys for grown-ups such as frog radios, frog telephones, frog lampstands and the like. But traditional craftsmen still produce true works of art – beautifully fashioned frogs of Murano glass from Italy or the hand-painted blue and white *azulejo* pottery from Portugal. And those who cannot resist the temptation of precious stones are amply catered to by jewellers who sell frogs in silver and, if expense is no object, solid gold or diamonds. Extraordinary treatment, indeed, for an extraordinary creature.

These two paper frogs are examples of the Japanese technique of origami. Opposite: frogs are featured on these stamps from Madagascar; and the silver paperweight depicts a mother frog proudly carrying a baby on her back.

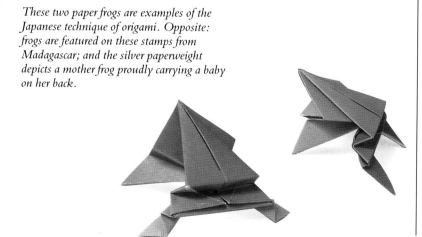

15

This inquisitive and endearing little frog, an Italian work in woodpulp, seems anxious to communicate a message. It would certainly be interesting to know something more about him and his pond companions.

Life and times of the frog

The males are the first to arrive. From May onward, they throng the ponds as the sun goes down, seeking their mates. After a quick glance around to make sure no intruders are present, they swell the vocal sacs situated on neck and throat and begin their nightly concert. Whether the croaking is loud or soft, rapid or measured, shrill or subdued, it has but one purpose: to reach the ears of the females and urge them to hurry to the breeding grounds. Once they arrive, there are no preliminaries or courtship rites. Each male grasps his partner from behind, just below the armpits, holding her tightly in the "amplexus" posture with his arms, furnished as they are with horny adhesive pads on the thumbs. The pair may stay in this position for hours, even all night, until spawning commences and the female is forced to expel her eggs. At that precise moment the male covers the eggs with sperm, fertilizing them, and releases his grip on her.

Even though fertilization is external (and this would seem inevitable since the male sex organs are hardly visible), this does not diminish the force of the passion involved in the vice-like embrace. In fact, it is virtually impossible to prise the two animals apart at this time. The eighteenth-century Italian biologist Lazzaro Spallanzani attempted to do so in one of his crueller experiments, and concluded that the male, even when whipped until he bleeds, will not release his mate until he is almost dying. Hunters of frogs, too, know from experience that it is relatively easy to catch a pair when they are clasped together in amplexus. Nevertheless, despite the risks they are running, frogs of all kinds continue to spawn in the light of the moon for as long as the summer nights permit.

These small amphibians of pond and swamp who croak in chorus to such delightful or disturbing effect (depending on your point of view) have been around for quite some time, certainly more than 100 million years. And perhaps the only thing to be said with certainty is that over the course of these centuries their musical repertory has not changed to any great extent. Indeed, the range is hardly extensive, restricted as it is to love serenades, rain choruses and alarm cries. Frogs, as

Frogs have been making music for hundreds of years. This terracotta ocarina, a simple wind instrument, is from the Alto Adige, a region in northern Italy. The frog opposite is merely pretending to sing. The little frog orchestra on the following pages is also from the Alto Adige.

already mentioned, are not violent creatures and are more often victims than hunters. So they are often called upon to defend themselves and may, in certain circumstances, behave quite heroically. Should they encounter a snake, for example, they will swell themselves with water like balloons, remaining exposed and otherwise helpless until their family has found safety. Such a tactic, though apparently threatening, is purely defensive, and a calculated risk. Experience shows that although they can emerge from such an encounter injured and bruised, or even dead, the chances are in favour of them surviving unscathed.

Frogs may not be aggressive, but they leave their rivals and enemies in no doubt as to their feelings if they are upset or frightened. The males, for example, are extremely possessive of the females and jealously guard their territory, even though they may only occupy it for a very short period. If, in the course of the breeding season, they are disturbed, they will let out angry, menacing cries, never forgetting, however, to keep a prudent distance between themselves and the intruder.

The defensive strategies of some frogs are even more strange

and astonishing. In the drier parts of Africa, the mottled burrowing frog (*Hemisus marmoratum*), having adopted the standard defensive attitude of swelling up like a balloon in face of danger, dives into the mud and digs out a deep, safe hole with its sharp snout and hind feet, hiding away until all is calm once more. And in Cameroon, the hairy frog (*Trichobatrachus robustus*), which lives in streams, derives its common name from the fact that during the breeding season it develops a hairy skin covering that helps it to survive this time of special stress and risk.

Odd in behaviour and curious in other ways as well: the frog lacks both a chest cavity and ribs. It breathes through its skin, and the rhythmic movement of the throat indicates that it is literally swallowing air through the nostrils. And the frog's vision is strangely limited, for its eyes will only detect objects that are moving very close to hand. This can lead to misunderstandings, as when one male comes across another male, but mistakes him for a female and makes a clumsy attempt to mount him. It may also result in a missed opportunity for feeding, as when a tasty morsel situated on a nearby rock or stone is ignored simply because it does not obligingly make a movement. In rare instances, too, the

No doubt about this one: the shell-covered monster, smacking rather of kitsch but certainly unusual, has surfaced from the depths of the swamp. Opposite: the ball-shaped frog from Russia, with its silky skin, is made from opalescent selenite.

This attractive blue frog is from China, fashioned in the ancient, elegant cloisonné technique, which fuses enamel and metal.

consequences of an error may prove fatal, should another frog be mistaken for an appetizing meal, which explains why frogs have gained the sinister reputation of being cannibals. Another strange fact is that frogs never drink. Their naked, defenseless skin is very delicate and highly permeable, absorbing water freely and needing to be kept constantly moist. So sun and ice are deadly enemies.

Given their unusual breeding habits, their vocal abilities and their extraordinary powers of survival, it is hardly surprising that frogs, from the beginning of time, have inspired a wealth of myth and superstition. They are celebrated far and wide as bringers of rain, heralds of spring, messengers of fortune and symbols of fertility. By reason of their amphibious nature and the fact that they spend much of their time resting or dormant, their moments of reawakening and reactivity are associated with the concepts of creation, rebirth and resurrection. In

Carved in stone by an African craftsman from Dahomey, this frog has a suitably sullen and weighty appearance.

ancient Egypt, scholars linked the frog to the miracles of nature, specifically to water and the primordial ocean, from which all things come, and, because of the large numbers of eggs laid, to abundance and fertility. Moreover, in the context of its longevity, its tenacity in withstanding storms, lack of food, absence of air and light, and, above all, its astonishing capacity to recover rapidly from wounds and injuries, the frog was equated with strength and vital energy. Consequently, it was enveloped in a haze of mystery that merely served to nourish countless beliefs associated with eternal life and the cult of the dead. It was not by chance, therefore, that the Egyptians mummified frogs; and it was for similar reasons that the Incas of Peru subsequently placed statuettes of frogs alongside corpses in tombs. Such customs naturally helped to feed the myth of their incredible resistance to the elements and extremes of climate, as well as their recuperative powers.

A multicoloured wooden frog from Bali. The symbolic figure of the frog appears frequently in the cultural and religious traditions of Indonesia, and particularly those of the island of Bali.

For all these reasons, figures of frogs, in all shapes and sizes, have long been believed to have the capacity to protect people against the evil eye, instil them with courage and cure them of disease. These beliefs are common to widely disparate cultures all over the world, both East and West, and were held in some parts of Europe until the nineteenth century. In many areas of Latin America, the frog featured in the armoury of witch doctors. The Mayas fashioned frog images from gold and from jade and emerald — green stones themselves reputed to possess magical properties — which took on superstitious, miraculous significance and were therefore worn as amulets around the neck to win love and friendship. Similarly, in medieval Europe, when the frog came to be associated with the Christian concept of resurrection, pendants and bracelets in its image were worn by rich and poor alike.

The vocal prowess of the male frog has also influenced popular lore and legend. Call it cheerful singing or lugubrious croaking, that noisy twilight chorus is taken as a sign of nature awakening from winter and from drought. Today, as in the past, country folk everywhere welcome the imminent arrival of spring, the promise of rain, the expectation of earth's abundance and the renewal of the life cycle. These hopes are reflected in an Indian hymn from the *Rigveda*, with the prayer: "May it please the frogs, during the many rains that sustain our cattle in their hundreds, to prolong our life!"

In Japan the frog is associated with good humour and happiness, as is emphasised in a seventeenth-century poem by Bashō:

> *"Breaking the silence*
> *Of an ancient pond,*
> *A frog jumped into water —*
> *A deep resonance."*

On the other side of the Yellow Sea, along the coasts and across the broad expanses of the Chinese countryside, the peasants, even today, observe the custom of placing frog-like idols in the rice fields as a propitiation for crops and a plea for rain. And in ancient Egypt, the singing of the frogs along the banks of the Nile was taken to be a veritable message of fertility.

To balance this positive outlook, there are quite a few stories that lay stress on the damage that frogs can do. The most famous of these, of course, is the passage from the Book of Exodus in the Bible which describes the second plague visited by God on the Egyptian Pharaoh in order to persuade

The black frog, carved in obsidian, with its beautiful pink ornamentation, is of Native American origin. Opposite: looking more like a toad, with improbably large ceramic feet, this is a product of Italian craftsmanship.

him to free the Israelites: "I will plague the whole of your territory with frogs … They shall come up from the river into your house, into your bedroom and on to your bed, into the houses of your courtiers and your people, into your ovens and your kneading troughs. The frogs shall clamber over you, your people and your courtiers …" The plague will end, and the frogs will die, only when the Pharaoh promises Moses and Aaron to obey God's command. (In fact, he breaks his promise and the Egyptians are subjected to swarms of flies and other plagues.)

There is, in fact, a logical explanation for the mythical showers of frogs that are said to have struck various regions at one time or another. They are simply caused by the first heavy rainstorms of the season which flood the burrows in swamps and marshes where frogs in their thousands have sought refuge against the drought. In the aftermath of the storm, these vast numbers of frogs, driven to the surface, are to be found crawling around in the mud, having materialized so suddenly that they seem to have fallen from the sky. Rather more disturbing, and less easily explained, are the modern

29

accounts of frogs showering down on city streets, as reported
to have occurred in Birmingham, England, and Naples and
San Remo in Italy. In the last case, local tradition advances the
theory, incredible as it may seem, that a violent storm carried
the animals bodily all the way from the shores of Africa.

A splendid Chinese poem tells of countless tiny eggs of frogs
falling from heaven and being deposited on the earth as dew.
No need of any scientific explanation here; it is simply a
matter of belief, abetted by a touch of imagination.

At other times, and in other lands, frogs have been credited

*Laughing fit to burst, these frogs on a
Japanese stamp play with a rabbit.
Opposite: the comical frog with a rather
astonished expression is actually a vase.
Following pages: two ceramic frog bookends.*

with a variety of attributes. In Japan, for instance, the word
kaeru means both "frog" and "return," and it is popularly
believed that frogs, even at a considerable distance from their
ponds, can easily find their way back. Based on this
assumption, it is logical that the frog should be chosen as the
protecting spirit of travellers.

Classical tradition also focuses on the role of frogs in private
and public life. Pliny asserted that a frog amulet would attract
love and friendship. In ancient Rome, where the frog had
countless admirers, it was the favourite animal of the divine
Venus, as it had been for her Greek counterpart, Aphrodite.
Venus, goddess of fertility, love and beauty, had her own good
reasons for making such a choice, but there was another valid
explanation, based on a phenomenon unique in the animal
world: frogs are born from a frothy, gelatinous egg mass, not
dissimilar to the foam of the sea from which Venus herself

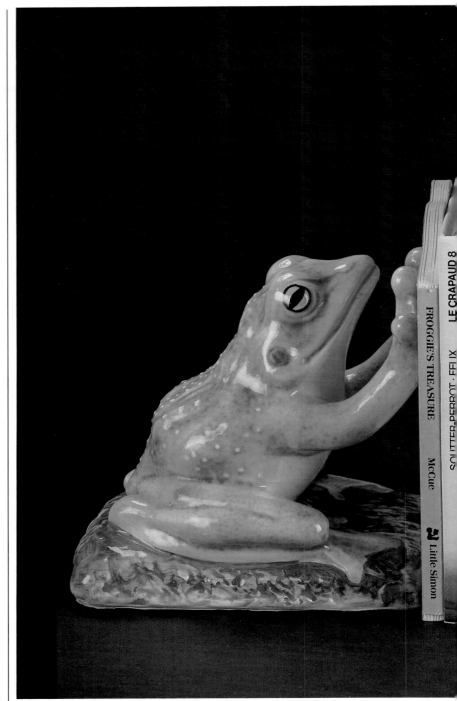

FROGGIE'S TREASURE McCue 📘 Little Simon

QUITTER · PERROT · FÉLIX LE CRAPAUD 8

FROGS

FROGS

HUTCHINSON

WH Allen

sprang. The goddess would certainly have approved of a frog from Central America, the túngara frog (*Physalaemus pustulosus*) which behaves very oddly indeed when it comes to fertilizing the female's eggs: using his hind legs, he stirs up the sticky fluid which she emits so as to make a nest for the young that has the appearance and consistency of whipped cream.

Throughout the Indonesian archipelago, frogs and toads occur in many guises – in temple sculptures, as decorative motifs in the beautiful dyed cloth technique known as *batik*, and as characters in certain elaborate dances from Bali. In one such dance, *The Toad on the Banana Tree*, the musical instruments, which accompany the movements of the dancers, produce a sound similar to the croaking of frogs and toads, while another performer recites the pantomime of the toad hunt. The two principal dancers impersonate the hunter and the prey, miming the encounter in a succession of spectacular jumps and turns. They size each other up, alternately retreating and advancing, until finally, building up to a tense, dramatic crescendo, the hunter leaps on his victim and makes the kill.

Associations with music are frequent in many cultures. Images of frogs are sometimes painted on drums, regarded as the guiding spirits of witch doctors and, when arranged in a circle, as a symbolic representation of the universe. The beating of the drums simulates the thunder with which the frog is associated, and the consequent arrival of the rains. For the Pima Indians of Arizona, however, the love calls of the frog inspire deeper feelings and wilder passions, as recounted by a young girl in this song:

> "*I ran, confused, to the pond*
> *Where I could hear the frogs singing.*
> *I ran, confused, to the pond,*

Where the frogs, clothed in bark, sang.
To the west roams the dragonfly,
Skimming the surface of the ponds,
Brushing it only with its tail,
Skimming it with quivering, rustling wings.
There, I ran as darkness fell,
Bearing cactus flowers in my hair.
There, I ran as darkness fell,
In the whispering night, to the place of song.''

The tree frogs, whose nocturnal croaking rivals that of their larger relatives in the breeding season, are equally evocative. But they have no need to resort to song when rain is in the offing. All that is necessary is to place the creature in a glass tank partially filled with water, with a miniature ladder for clambering in and out. Rainy or settled conditions may be predicted according to whether the frog decides to sit inside or outside the tank.

Many of the true frogs are of course distinguished by another feature: their capacity for jumping. Two American species, the bullfrog and the leopard frog are veritable high-class athletes. Females of the former species are up to 8 in (20 cm) long, and males 7 in (18 cm); the latter, is smaller, but has a swifter cat-like leap. Both have been immortalized in the pages of Mark Twain, although it is the bullfrog that is the real undisputed hero of his story and long-jump champion of the county of Calaveras. In fact, frog-leaping competitions, involving both species, are common in the United States.

Unfortunately, the fame of the bullfrog is not confined to jumping, for its flesh is considered very tasty, and the creatures are caught in their thousands, many of them eventually to be served up in fashionable restaurants. In some communities, however, pregnant women are prohibited from eating them as they believe the unborn child might decide to start hopping about in the womb.

Contrary to appearances, this red wooden frog from Southeast Asia is really a box with a small flap in the back. Opposite: a rather plump green and yellow frog, made of papier mâché, from the Indian city of Srinagar.

Royal treatment

As with chicken and egg, so with frog and tadpole. Which came first? Well, science has no plausible answer to this question, and of course no adult is even qualified to venture an opinion. For, as every child knows, the correct reply is neither. In the beginning it was a prince, or even a princess. Traditional folklore and fairy tale attest to this simple truth. Consider, for example, this version.

Once upon a time there was a princess who, while playing one day, accidentally dropped a golden ball into the depths of a well. Her desperate weeping attracted the attention of a frog. Hopping up to her, he offered to retrieve the ball, but on one condition: the princess must agree to live with him and learn to love him, sealing such love with a kiss. The princess readily accepted the offer, though in her heart she felt there was no way in which a frog could live with a human being. Indeed, as soon as the frog had returned the golden ball to her, she

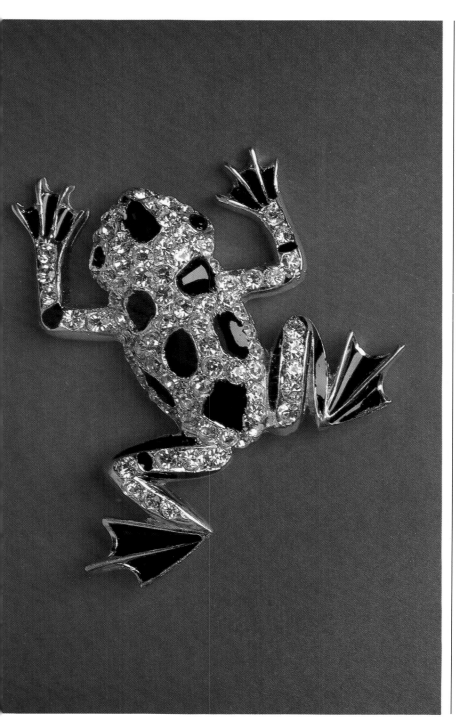

Two stamps, from West and East, depict the familiar theme of the frog prince or king. Arab culture has often originated the archetypes which have subsequently found their way into popular Western tradition.

grabbed it and ran off back to the castle. By the following day the princess had completely forgotten both the frog and her promise, but when dinner time came, she was astonished to find the frog already seated at the royal table. Flushed with confusion and guilt, she leapt to her feet and fled from the hall, commanding the servants to throw the creature out immediately. This done, she returned and sat down in her place as if nothing had happened.

The king, her father, astonished at her agitation and strange behaviour, asked her the reason, and she dared not lie to him. She told him the whole story, including her vow to the frog. Angrily, he rebuked her: "Do not scorn someone who has helped you," he thundered; and he made her promise to carry out the conditions of the contract. For three weeks the princess lived with the frog. Little by little she came to like the ugly creature, but all the same she could not conceal her physical revulsion whenever they met. So when the frog reminded her that she had promised to give him a kiss, she did so with teeth tightly clenched; and straight afterwards, consumed by rage, she grabbed hold of the little animal and hurled him violently against the wall. But by now the deed was done, however much she wished it otherwise, the kiss had been bestowed. And thus, instead of dying as a result of smashing into the wall, lo and behold, the frog was miraculously transformed into a prince. And what is more, an extremely handsome one.

"An evil witch cast a wicked spell on me, transforming me into that disgusting creature," explained the youth to the pleasantly surprised princess, "but now your love has broken the magic and I am restored to my true self." So, as fate clearly

decreed, the princess married her frog prince and they lived, in traditional fairy-tale fashion, happily ever after.

The tale of the Frog Prince has been told in many versions, suitably adapted to the culture and custom of different lands, and it remains one of the perennial childhood favourites. But there is another legend, equally cosmopolitan, and likewise concerned with ponds, water lilies and castles, which alters the balance of the sexes. The following version is based on the traditional Russian tale.

Once upon a time there was a tsar who had three sons. One fine day he called them to him and told them each to shoot an arrow from his silver bow: each son would find a wife where the arrow landed. Two of the arrows fell in the courtyards of great castles and thus two of the sons married beautiful princesses. But the arrow shot by Ivan, the youngest, a shy and awkward boy, fell into a pond. It was picked up by a frog, who

Two more stamps, one German, the other Dutch, pay tribute to the dual nature of the fairy-tale frog and its splendid and regal transformation from animal to human.

naturally claimed the right to marry the lad. Poor Ivan had no choice: he had to take the frog as his wife.

Of course, matters did not end there. The old tsar had the brilliant idea of testing the qualities of his three daughters-in-law to decide which of them deserved to be the future tsarina: the position would go to the one who wove the finest cloth, cooked the tastiest pie and embroidered the prettiest cushion. Contrary to predictions, Ivan's wife came first in all three categories: in the dead of night, unknown to her husband, the frog princess had shed her animal skin and, assisted by her maidservants, had woven, cooked and embroidered veritable masterpieces. At this point, the tsar, somewhat dismayed at the prospect of leaving his throne to a son with a wife who, for all her skills, could hardly be described as attractive, decided to stake everything and announced officially that his successor would be the son who brought the most beautiful and elegant wife to the great ball at the castle.

Ivan, already amazed and bewildered by everything that had

so far happened, was devastated by this news. But his gentle
frog-wife comforted him: "Go fearlessly to the ball and I will
join you later; you shall see the throne will be yours." Hardly
convinced, but given no alternative, Ivan followed her advice.
And he was more astonished than anyone when halfway
through the evening, his frog princess made a grand entrance
into the ballroom, but transformed into a charming girl, by far
the loveliest of all. Ivan, beaming with joy, could not
understand how this had happened; so he furtively rushed
home to see if he could throw any more light on the matter.
And there on the bed, to his great surprise, lay the discarded
frog skin of his wife. "So that's the secret!" exclaimed Ivan;
and determined to rid himself forever of this intolerable
situation, he tossed the skin into the fire. If only he had not
done that! The princess, on her return from the ball, was
distraught, and with good reason: "Without my frog skin, the
spell that binds me compels me to flee far away and never to
return, unless you have the courage and strength to overcome
the hardest trials to save me from my sad destiny." Could Ivan
leave his wife to such a fate? Certainly not. And off he went to
win her back for good. There is no space here to describe in
detail the terrifying adventures that the boy, no longer shy and
awkward, had to endure. Suffice it to say that at the end, he

*Frogs inspire both humour and ingenuity, as
exemplified by the well-bred gentleman
sitting in his rocking chair, studying his
stocks and shares, and, opposite, by the
candleholder-frog with his golden crown.*

A charming little carving in bone, from Ladak in India, of a frog and twins clinging to her back: not a particularly realistic picture, but a tender evocation of maternal love.

found his beloved frog princess imprisoned in a dark cell at the top of a tower. And having discovered her at last, he received the answer to all his anxious questions: "A wicked baba-yaga cast a terrible spell on me," said the princess, "but now your love has freed me forever from her magic." So, again in true fairy-tale tradition, the pair lived happily ever after. Just as in the other story where the frog was a dashing prince. So there is no real distinction here between male and female. In either case the handsome prince or radiant princess has been placed under a terrible spell, thus appearing in the guise of a slimy little animal which inspires only disgust and repulsion. And the moral is, of course, that only a great act of love can reverse the situation, breaking the curse and enabling all concerned to live

in lasting happiness and contentment.

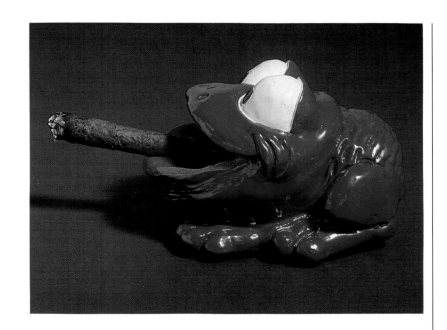

In total contrast, this frog from the islands of the Caribbean, painted in brilliant green clay, is the very epitome of masculine swagger, complete with outsize cigar.

The kiss, love's ultimate and infallible therapy, alone possesses the power of regeneration.

Probably the most famous of all fairy tales focusing on the subject of romance and marriage between humans and animals is *Beauty and the Beast*, and the many tales of frogs, princes and princesses that have persisted over the centuries are variations on this theme of an incompatible relationship between fair and foul and often, by implication, virtue and vice. All these stories culminate in the wondrous transformation of the ugly, repulsive animal into a handsome human. Misunderstanding and misery give way to reconciliation and lasting happiness.

The different versions of what is essentially the same tale invariably present the disguised hero or heroine as the victim of a wicked spell cast by a witch (or a baba-yaga); but none of

Folk Song
Mr Froggie went a-co
Sword and pistol by
le went to Mis
e a loud

them offer any explanation as to what has incurred such wrath in the first place. There is no hint of provocation and just retribution. The individual who is freed from the spell is so obviously virtuous and beautiful, both physically and spiritually, that it is quite implausible that he or she could previously have been a bad person meriting punishment. Good and evil are, in fact, clearly defined from the beginning. The motivation of the witch, therefore, is personal and irrational.

So the frog is represented as the victim, but the fairy tale never explains how and why things happened as they did. The reader is left to guess and interpret events at will. Perhaps the witch is determined to revenge someone associated with the royal children affected by the spell, maybe their parents, monarchs who refused to do her bidding. Or perhaps the motive impelling the witch to pronounce the fateful formula

The bronze frog, above, is certainly a chatterer, probably giving all and sundry the benefit of his wisdom, quite unlike the passive little fellow in silver crouched on top of a thimble, opposite. As for the group of frog stationery accessories on the preceding pages, they seem all at sixes and sevens.

that turns lovely children into frogs is envy, no more or less – envy which, though it can cause suffering, is destined to be vanquished by its very opposite: love.

The legend of the frog prince goes back a long way and has been passed down by oral and written tradition, with one text dating from the thirteenth century. The best known anthology in which the tale appears is that of the Brothers Grimm in 1813. But no matter the place and time, every version depicts the frog as the personification of generosity, common sense and wisdom – qualities that are ageless and enduring.

The fables of Aesop, a shadowy figure from ancient Greece who is thought to have lived in the fourth century B.C., have been retold in a number of recent collections. They are short tales, each making a clear moral point. One of them tells of two frogs on a hot summer's day who are basking quietly in

Legends and fairy tales, myths and magic featuring frogs are to be found all over the world, including Celtic mythology, as seen in this terracotta frog with the wide eyes and rude grimace, wearing the classic hat of Merlin the Wizard.

the sun when they are overcome by an incredible thirst. They decide to set out together to look for water. When they come to a deep well, they discuss whether or not to jump in. One of the frogs thinks they should dive in, because the water looks so clear and nobody is likely to disturb them down there. But the other warns him: "If we jump into the well, how are we going to get out?" The moral, of course, is never to let oneself be tempted by appearances but to be guided by prudence in order to avoid danger.

Another of Aesop's fables with a very clear moral concerns a group of young rascals who are playing around a pond. Their favourite game turns out to be aiming stones at any frogs who poke their heads above the surface. This goes on for a while until all the frogs in the pond are terrified. Eventually, however, the oldest and most respected frog leaps up on to a lily pad and addresses the lads severely: "You are enjoying yourselves and give no thought to the consequences of what you are doing. For you it is just a game, but for us frogs it means death!"

Of all Aesop's frog fables, the most famous is surely that of the conceited, swaggering little creature who must prove at any cost that he is the equal of an ox. To show off his strength and power he begins to swell himself up: he puffs and puffs and puffs until, in the end, he bursts. The moral: pride goes before a fall.

Today the frog remains as popular as ever in children's books, animated cartoons and, especially, on television. *The Muppet Show* proved a worldwide success, and its compere, the

affable, easy-going glove puppet, Kermit, is an acknowledged star of the small screen, appealing to young and old alike with his subtle blend of vulnerability, optimism and charm.

Kermit may have more entertainment value than universal meaning but throughout history the frog has been recognized for his wider significance. In Southeast Asia, for example, he is the symbol of fertility, and a frog made of semi-precious stones is sometimes presented to a newly married couple as an augury of numerous and healthy children. In ancient Egypt, on the other hand, the frog portrayed on the head of the idol symbolized the embryonic state of the cereal grain which, after decomposition, would begin to sprout once more. And it was the frog that every morning watched and ensured the sunrise.

Ugly but nice could be the description of this amusing little crouching frog in multicoloured ceramic.

In some popular traditions, to dream of a frog is to be surrounded by people of an indiscreet nature; but in Japan it is a promise of strength and perseverance. There is a widespread custom in Burma of giving newborn babies a small figure of a golden frog as an amulet against the evil eye of the devil. In India the frog plays a part in all the principal religious rituals; and the Native Americans and Australian Aborigines both use the singing of frogs as a weather barometer.

Frogs have a central role, too, at the Carnival time preceding Lent. The town of Hertogenbosch, capital of the province of North Brabant in the Netherlands, observes a custom dating back to the Middle Ages. During their three days of Carnival, the elected frog prince has complete freedom

The brightly-coloured pattern on the head and back of this small frog, carved of grey stone, might be a mysterious symbol of wisdom and fertility

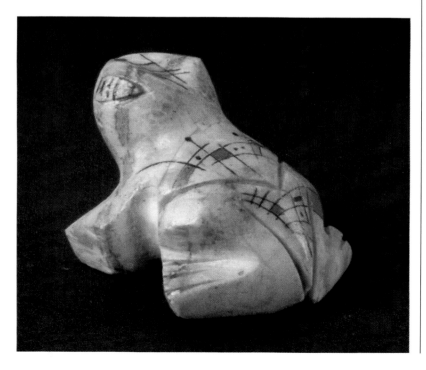

to go anywhere and drink as much he wants. The town is decorated with posters and paintings of frogs, and frog images are worn on all hats and coats.

On a somewhat sadder note, there is an ancient belief that under the slimy skin of a frog is concealed the soul of a dead child. It is bad luck, therefore to kill a frog.

Yet another ancient legend stresses the importance of learning to listen to the croaking of frogs in the right frame of mind. One evening a monk was kneeling at prayer when he was disturbed by the sound of a croaking frog. No matter how hard he tried, he was unable to ignore the noise, so much so that he opened the window and shouted at the frog to stop the din and respect the hour of prayer. The monk was reputed to be holy, and all living creatures were therefore accustomed to obeying him without question: animals of woodland, farmyard, barn and burrow were obliged to fall silent so that the good father could say his prayers in peace. But now, no sooner had he regained his concentration than he was

interrupted yet again. This time it was an inner voice

insisting that perhaps the frog's croaking was just as pleasing to God as were his own psalms.

The monk, nevertheless, put the thought aside. How could God possibly find any beauty in the cry of a frog? And he went back to his praying. But the inner voice interrupted him once more: why then did God create the frog and furnish it with a croak? At this point the monk decided to show an open mind. He went to the window again and listened carefully to the rhythmical song of the frog, accompanied now by all the frogs in the neighbourhood. And this time he heard no discordant din but a melodious chorus, enhanced and embellished by the silence of the night. He felt in harmony with the whole universe and, for the first time in his life, the holy man knew the real meaning of prayer.

The little flower-patterned Indian box, below, shows a frog and a snake confronting each other. The brooch, opposite, is of Oriental craftsmanship, but frog ornaments of this type are also worn in the West, for example in Hertogenbosch during Carnival time.

Hidden depths

For all its princely nature – which might argue some right of privilege – the gentle frog of fairy tale has not been spared the attentions of the psychoanalysts. Sigmund Freud, it is true, did not scrutinize this animal in particular for hidden meanings, but his neglect is perhaps understandable; Freud simply never had enough time, in the material sense, to carry all his work (frogs included) through to its logical conclusions. But the father of psychoanalysis had the comfort of knowing that his legacy was in good hands; having explained how and why fairy tales should be interpreted, it was left to his disciples to enlarge on his theory and to continue exploring and analyzing this aspect of the subconscious mind along the lines he had laid down.

The theme of fairy-tale analysis was developed in particular by one of Freud's most loyal followers, Bruno Bettelheim, who was born in Vienna and later settled in the United States.

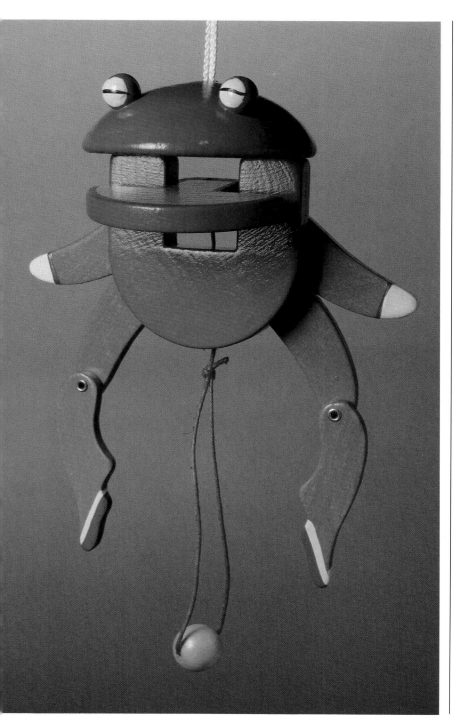

Lecturer in psychology and psychiatry at the University of Chicago, Bettelheim was for almost thirty years director of the Orthogenic School for psychotic children. He was also the author of *Uses of Enchantment*, a key work in the analytic interpretation of fairy tales. A whole chapter of this book is devoted to the frog or, more specifically, to the tale of the *Frog King*, one of the several versions of the frog prince/king fable which we have already mentioned.

As an analyst, Bettelheim is naturally concerned with the deeper meaning of the story. The princess, he points out, weeps not only for the loss of her ball but also for the lost innocence of her childhood. The ugly frog alone can restore

The beautifully transparent tones of the pink-grey quartz used to fashion this frog from Thailand create an impression of delicacy and lightness.

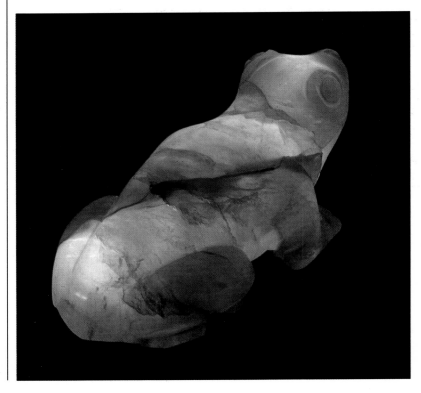

the ball, in other words perfection, to her, rescuing it from the darkness – symbol of her psyche – into which it has fallen. To get what she wants, the girl is prepared to make a promise, without thought of the possible consequences. And when the frog claims his due, the princess slams the door in his face. But now the super-ego, in the guise of the father-king, intervenes. The more the princess tries to deny the frog's demands, the more the king insists she honour them in full. What has begun as a game has become extremely serious: the princess has to grow up, and is compelled to carry out the task she has undertaken.

All very well; but so far only the princess has been

Even in the fairy tale of the Frog King, *everything seems perfectly normal, as does this metallic representation of the animal on its floating leaf, but then ...*

mentioned. What of the frog and the part he plays in this sequence of events? In terms of psychoanalysis, what does he represent? Bettelheim has no doubts: he is the child who needs to grow up, who for the first time discovers sex and subconsciously is afraid of it. And as traditionally the frog can never be described as a reckless animal, the role as a timid child is particularly appropriate. Like the princess, the frog, according to Bettelheim, has to mature before any union between the two is possible. Like any child, the frog craves a life that is wholly symbiotic. Although he wishes to stay in bed with his mother, she has to throw him out, just as the frog is thrown out of bed and freed from the spell that binds him to his immature existence.

Bettelheim puts it bluntly and clearly. For him, the frog is simply a symbol of sex. He goes further, pointing out that at a preconscious level, a child connects the sticky, slimy sensations aroused in him by the frog (or the toad) with sensations associated with his sexual organs. The frog's capacity to swell himself up when stimulated has associations, albeit unconsciously, with the erectile properties of the penis. So no matter how repellent the frog may seem, as vividly described in this fairy tale, we are assured that even an ugly, slippery creature such as this will be transformed into something marvellous, provided everything proceeds in the right way and at the right time. The story, whilst admitting, like any child, that the frog (or whatever animal is concerned) is repugnant, wins the trust of the child and implants in him the firm certainty that when the time is ripe this repulsive frog will turn out to be the most delightful life companion. And this

This porcelain mother frog, with its decorative pattern in relief, has a comfortable, reassuring air. The little girl, opposite, can claim to be a frogman in all respects, complete with mask, snorkel and flippers.

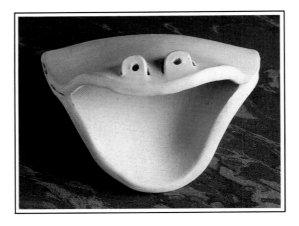

The terracotta frog, above, is all eyes and mouth. Opposite: Jeremy Fisher, one of Beatrix Potter's famous characters, is seen here resting after a day's fishing. Three bathroom frogs are depicted on the preceding pages; the soap holder is of German design.

message, insists Bettelheim, is transmitted without any direct reference to anything sexual.

Whilst on the subject of sex, it is worth recalling that in another well-known fairy tale, *Sleeping Beauty*, it is a frog that predicts that the queen, who is desperate at not having conceived, will become a mother within a year. At least that is the queen's version, but some commentators on the story suggest that this frog is really a dashing youth in disguise whose role is not confined to making a prophecy but plays a much more positive and active part in the proceedings. In fact, he actually helps the queen realize her dream of motherhood, succeeding where the king, her husband, perhaps worn out by affairs of the state, has so far failed.

Why, then, among all woodland animals, should the frog, and sometimes the related toad, be chosen as a symbol of sex? Bettelheim goes on to explain that in comparison with the lion

or other wild beasts, the frog (or toad) does not excite fear, being an animal that in no way poses any threat. Viewed in a negative light, it must inspire a feeling of disgust. So it is hard to imagine a better way, argues Bettelheim, to show a child that there is nothing to fear from what appear to be repugnant aspects of sex.

This is the opinion of Bettelheim, a faithful disciple of the father of psychoanalysis and hence an orthodox Freudian. But investigators of the subconscious mind who subscribe to the Jungian school also accord the frog ample consideration.

Carl Gustav Jung himself gave some thought to the animal

*A couple of very handsome Chinese frogs in
brightly-enamelled metal, well aware of
being symbols in psychoanalysis, chat
together about the day's events on the pond.*

and mentioned it on several occasions, emphasizing two
fundamental features. Above all, he saw the frog as a
transitional creature, an amphibian living indifferently on
water or dry land, born as a tadpole and transformed into an
adult of entirely different appearance and structure. In other
words, the frog symbolizes for the subconscious a transitional
phase halfway between an aquatic, and hence more primitive,
dimension and a terrestrial, and thus more conscious,
dimension. Secondly, insists Jung, although the frog is
phylogenetically a primitive, cold-blooded animal, it possesses
certain morphological and structural features that are very

similar to those of humans. Consider, for example, the front legs, which closely resemble tiny arms and hands. It is no accident that children are led instinctively to look at the frog in human terms, more so than any other cold-blooded creature. The theme of transformation and anthropomorphism is also fundamental to the fairy tales of frog princes and princesses.

Marie-Louise von Franz, a pupil of Jung, and one of the principal exponents of analytical psychology, has done important work on popular legend and folklore, and has submitted some interesting interpretations on the deeper meaning of fairy tales. On many occasions, and above all in one of her most famous books, *Introduction to the Interpretation of Fairy Tales*, she has analyzed the Russian tale of the frog princess from a symbolic perspective. In a general context, the

princess represents the Anima. This is, in fact, the term used by Jung, in contrast to Animus, to indicate the unconscious feminine component of the male personality. According to Jung, the Anima is the archetype of life itself, but as for all archetypes, there is an ambivalence: it may possess a man and transform him in a negative, involutional sense, unless correctly understood and interpreted; or it may assume positive significance, provided it is recognized as such and transformed by individual experience. Von Franz suggests that the frog princess, as Anima, represents the gift of poetic fantasy, the capacity to create the symbolic forms of life. If, therefore, the hero sets fire to the skin, the gesture shows a relationship with creative reality that is too analytical, impulsive and passionate. In order to succeed in winning his wife back, the tsar's son must throw off his immature, clumsy and timid attitude and must find the courage to overcome the most demanding trials. Only thus, by means of a difficult and laborious process, will man finally become mature and re-establish a proper relationship with his Anima.

It is by now quite clear that in order to represent this theme of transition and transformation in symbolic terms, there could be no more suitable animal than the frog, capable as it is of remarkable evolution from a primitive, aquatic tadpole to a terrestrial, anthropomorphic animal.

A pair of frogs in strongly contrasting mood. The green bathing beauty is from Germany, the serious professor with his pipe, opposite, is from England in the 1940s.

This severe figure in Java stone clearly commands a good deal of respect, and quite rightly, since frogs have been exploited over the centuries for a variety of purposes, culinary and pharmaceutical: numbers are declining and it is high time thought was given to saving the endangered species.

Remedies and recipes

Beautiful and deadly, the South American dyeing poison dart frog (*Dendrobates tinctorius*) secretes in its skin a poisonous substance capable of killing its most dangerous enemy within a few minutes. The local Indians, who know the animal and its properties, take advantage of it. They catch it, run it through with a sharp stick and quite dispassionately roast it over a slow flame until they have collected all the poison necessary for tipping the points of their deadly arrows. They have been doing this for centuries.

Modern medicine, on the other hand, uses this poison to treat various ailments, including heart disease. Nor is that all. The skin of a frog is a veritable mine of drugs. It contains both natural antibiotics and several substances, such as cerulein, that are capable of soothing the most severe forms of biliary colic and have proved to be valuable in treating some painful tumours; moreover, experiments have been carried out to test

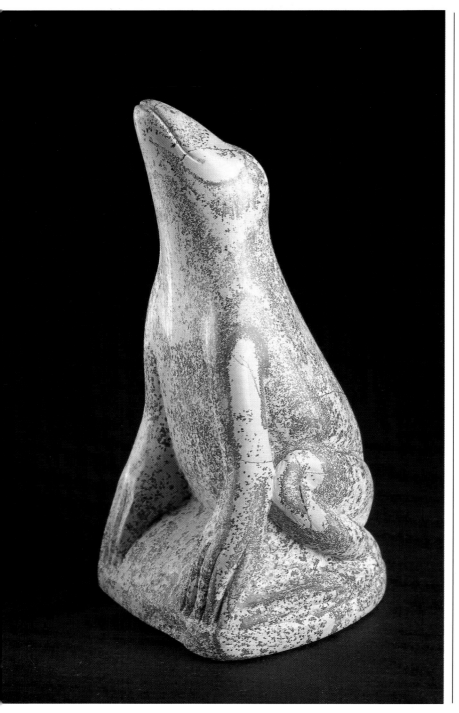

their effectiveness against drug addiction and AIDS. The tadpoles, too, secrete a hormone that can cure gastric ulcers. Strange animals indeed; no wonder some people regard them as enchanted.

Indeed, there is very little of the frog that cannot be used to some end. Skin, flesh, bones and venom have been utilized for centuries, all over the world, for a variety of purposes, worthy and unworthy: in science and medicine, in magic and *haute cuisine*.

In Italy, for example, during the early nineteenth century, there were those who believed that eye and nose infections could be cured by tying a live frog to the head. Pellegrino Artusi, a chef of international renown, recommended anyone suffering from chest or intestinal trouble to drink a refreshing bowl of frog soup, and prescribed frog meat for delicate

The frog ashtray has a peaceful, almost seraphic appearance. But the modern Chinese frog in cornelian, opposite, on its classical stand of wood, looks more animated, a little haughty perhaps.

constitutions. But long before that, in Roman times, frogs, either alive or dead, baked or boiled, were considered to be remedies against all kinds of sickness. Even Pliny the Elder advocated applying part of a frog's back to the head of a patient.

Such theories prompted the appearance of popular handbooks full of unusual, often outlandish, recipes. One of these, a remedy for fever, recommended drowning a frog in oil and massaging the body with the ointment thus obtained, not forgetting meanwhile to pop the dead animal under the clothing and wear it as an amulet. Another prescription, intended to heal skin irritations, was to take several newborn frogs, reduce them to ashes and then to breathe this aroma slowly through the nose. For toothache the ideal remedy was to rinse the mouth with the soup obtained from frog boiled in vinegar, while for arthritis two or three frogs, as need dictated, should be applied to the painful parts.

For magic potions obtained from parts of the frog, what could be more apt than scales such as these, with six Chinese statuettes of cast iron in varying sizes? Actually these scales were used for weighing opium.

These bizarre recipes were based more on superstition than on proven pharmaceutical properties. So it is hardly surprising that such elaborate concoctions should be more earnestly commended for their magical rather than therapeutic qualities. Above all, they were valued more for their assumed efficacy in resolving difficult and complex matters of the heart (in the romantic sense) than for the chemical properties exploited nowadays by science.

Here, for instance, is a recipe for an infatuated girl. Do you have a loved one who does not return your affection? Never fear: all you need do is resort to a little witchcraft. Sacrifice the life of a frog by sticking it through with pins while still alive; shut it in a box and leave it to die and dry out, then remove one of its key-shaped bones. Now comes the clever part. Stitch the bone into the coat of your unsuspecting victim and your efforts will soon be rewarded: give it a week and the man of your dreams will be mad with love and ready to satisfy your every desire.

Even so, it is not always guaranteed that spells and charms will work as expected. There is a story dating from the sixth century of a lady who, in order to poison her husband, already stricken with heart trouble, decided to give him a frog to eat. Having fed him this titbit in a tasty soup, she was surprised, and doubtless greatly disappointed, to find that instead of killing him, it cured him in a trice. What had happened was something that the woman, unaware of the real pharmaceutical powers of the frog, could not possibly have imagined: the extraordinary substances contained in the skin of the frog had activated the heart of the invalid and restored his health.

Men can also profit from using spells. Do you want to find out whether a woman is truthful? Wait until she is asleep and place a frog's tongue on her breast. Then, but only then, begin questioning her about things that concern you. She will answer everything without lying. At least this is the advice of Democritus; and even today there are those who will resort to

A frog-shaped jug, in which the watery characteristics of both animal and object are skilfully conveyed.

magic, though not necessarily this particular strategy, in similar circumstances.

The three witches in Shakespeare's *Macbeth*, huddled at midnight, in thunder and lightning, around their boiling cauldron, include "eye of newt, and toe of frog" among the ingredients of their sinister brew, testifying to the fact that even the practitioners of sorcery acknowledged frogs to possess magical properties. Significantly, however, the weird sisters select another animal as their main ingredient:

> *"Toad, that under cold stone*
> *Days and nights has thirty one*
> *Swelter'd venom sleeping got,*
> *Boil thou first i' the charmed pot."*

Shakespeare, well versed in the popular superstitions of his

*This fine antique bronze from Java, by
comparison with its companion, opposite, is
squat and ugly, but there is room in the pond
for all sorts.*

day, recognized that the toad, unjustly maligned for its ugly
and sinister appearance, was traditionally associated with the
ill-omened universe of witches and demons. The creature was
advertised as an excellent remedy by itinerant quack doctors
and tooth extractors who played on the gullibility of simple
folk at country fairs, peddling their medicines and potions; and
in many a horror and ghost story it was served up at table as a
lethal delicacy.

As already mentioned, frogs and toads are very different in
appearance, and easily distinguishable; moreover, frogs have
popularly been endowed with positive attributes, and toads
with negative qualities. Yet not only are they frequently
confused, but their legendary and mythical roles are often
reversed. Thus, although in medieval Christianity the frog was
hailed as the symbol of resurrection, it was simultaneously
represented, together with the toad, as a diabolical creature. In

apocalyptic tradition, for example, the unclean spirits spewed from the mouth of the infernal dragon took the form of frogs.

For its part, the toad, customarily reviled, was often regarded as the propitiary deity of rain; and it, too, especially in ancient Egypt, had associations with the cult of the dead.

It is quite impossible to distinguish the two animals in the sixteenth- and seventeenth-century illustrations of witches' kitchens. But the distinction is much more clear-cut when we consider the history of what might, in the circumstances, be described as normal gastronomy. Here the preference has always been exclusively for frogs. And if we think that this

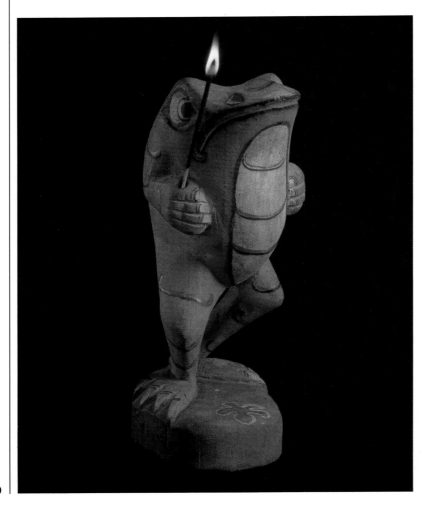

*The frog-shaped belt buckle is American,
and strictly practical. The frog from Bali,
opposite, is an incense burner: together with
the perfumed smoke, it has an air of magic
about it.*

form of gluttony is a comparatively recent phenomenon, it is worth recalling that frogs and tadpoles were both habitually eaten by the Aztecs of Montezuma's court, raised and consumed like fish by medieval monks, and regarded as a great delicacy by gourmets such as Lorenzo the Magnificent, who relished the frogs' legs served in the humblest inns of the Tuscan countryside.

By and large, the prospect is far from encouraging. Slaughtered in the interests of *haute cuisine*, sacrificed wholesale for scientific experiment, decimated by pollution thanks to the fact that their naked, ultra-sensitive skin reacts immediately to any atmospheric change, many populations of frogs and toads face the likelihood of extinction. From Europe to California and Australia, the uncanny and disturbing silence that hovers over ponds and swamps on summer nights ought to serve as a warning to us all.

Art imitating nature

The frog family contains its oddities. The marsupial tree frog *Gastrotheca ovifera* from South America, for example, has strange bony bulges on the head which make it look like a miniature prehistoric monster. And as so often happens, art imitates nature, dreaming up fantastic creations to give form and substance to thought and feeling, to accentuate with brutal realism the defects and horrors of human folly, to make an ironic comment on systems and philosophies. Monsters may be fashioned or depicted in an attempt to resolve the many enigmas of human existence. They may be intended to disturb and to shock, or they may simply whet the imagination.

There was a time when frogs and toads served to inspire a whole range of fantastic and visionary images in sculpture and painting, many of which somehow symbolized the transition from the fast-receding darkness of medieval cosmology to the dawn of a new, enlightened age. The most original exponent

of moral allegory in fifteenth-century painting, often assuming grotesque forms, half-human, half-animal, was the Dutch painter Hieronymus Bosch. One of his works depicts a helmet in the guise of a frog; and among his extraordinary collection of animals, life-like frogs and toads assume allegorical significance. There is a risk, however, as we revel in these paintings, with their infinite variety of forms and combinations, of seeing hidden objects and meanings everywhere, even where they do not exist. The ambiguities and complexities of his rebuses, in which imagination runs riot, are sometimes deceptive. But not always. The figure that emerges from the plate of the Negro in *The Temptation of St Anthony* is undoubtedly a frog with the head of an old man, and it represents the attainment of the highest level of human wisdom. And the demon lasciviously stretched out beside the temptation of lust, waiting for her cup to be filled with a love

These two small objects from Asia stand midway between craft and art. The Nepalese frog, above, is made of semi-precious stones, copper and brass; the one from Burma, opposite, is carved from an unusually coloured stone.

philter, is certainly a toad. So, too, is the figure that lies on the breast of a woman punished for her vanity, among those consigned to hell in *The Garden of Earthly Delights*; and likewise the animal painted as an emblem of pride and arrogance on the standard of the horseman condemned to eternal damnation, along with all his companions.

Yet Bosch does not confine himself to attributing the toad with the major sins of lust, vanity and pride. In accordance with conventions of his time, he considers the toad to be wholly evil: indeed, in his triptych of *The Hay-Wain*, which hangs in the Prado, he depicts the fallen angels consigned forever to the infernal abyss along with a crowd of horrible toad–demons. And, adopting the same symbol of evil and avarice, Pieter Bruegel the Elder, in his painting *The Fall of the Rebel Angels*, portrays the toad as a veritable monster, so much so that he finds it unnecessary to mask the creature in order to

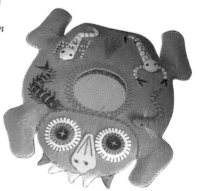

These modern products may not be of great value but they are certainly amusing. The timid frog with a built-in mirror comes from Bali, and the frog-jug, opposite, is from England. The clockwork tin and plastic jumping frogs on the preceding pages are Italian.

underline its immortality and greed: its very appearance is enough. Even naturalists of the period were convinced of the toad's miserly qualities. It was said, in fact, that the toad fed on soil, but did not have to eat more than it could hold with its foot so that its food supply would never run out. Furthermore, it even slept with some soil in its mouth, the motive again being sheer greed and anxiety lest anyone steal it from him.

In Latin America, on the other hand, where the toad was worshipped, together with the frog, as a divinity, the emphasis was always on its allegedly magical properties. The fact that various drugs, medicines and potions were often stored in earthenware pots fashioned in the guise of these creatures was believed to render them all the more effective.

In Peru, examples of Mohican art include pots and vases in animal forms, which were once thought to be associated with fertility symbols, but are now believed to have been used by the Matsa tribe of the Amazon to store a hallucinogenic substance derived from frogs' glands. The effect of this, when drunk, was to sharpen the senses sufficiently to permit direct communication with the natural world.

In general, however, artists and craftsmen looked on the frog, rather than the toad, for inspiration, and for its broad range of positive rather than negative attributes. First and foremost were the animal's associations with sexuality and childbirth. This close connection was recognized by many

89

ancient cultures and illustrated in bronze and earthenware artefacts, combining art, myth and popular superstition. A statue of Greco-Egyptian origin shows a frog supporting a woman in a sensual, provocative pose, who in her turn bears on her shoulders the protective god of childbirth, Bes. Closer to modern times, a late sixteenth-century representation of the goddess Aphrodite, in silver, shows her crouched on the back of a huge amphibian, holding Eros above her.

Linked more explicitly to the sexual act, the frog often appears in art as a participant in erotic, phallic cults. Thus in one example it is shown being straddled by a monstrous pygmy with mocking, animal-like features. Goya, too, was familiar with the frog and its specifically feminine symbolic connotations. He was fascinated by the visionary realm of Bosch, with its enigmatic monsters, but his own pictorial analysis shifted the emphasis to the relationship of dream and

The plump litle croaking frog in blue ceramic comes from the Bugis tribe of Celebes, while the piece of jewellery, opposite, is Colombian.

reality, the conscious and the unconscious. One of his engravings shows a woman in front of her mirror, appalled and dismayed at her transformation into a frog with human looks, dimensions and attributes. But if art has unequivocally stressed the affinity between frog and woman in the dual role of lover and mother, it has also pointed to the analogies that exist with the universe of children.

The frog has traditionally been envisaged as protecting and assisting in childbirth, and the cries of newborn babies have often been compared to the plaintive croaks of the small pond dwellers. In the sixteenth century a printer from Zurich,

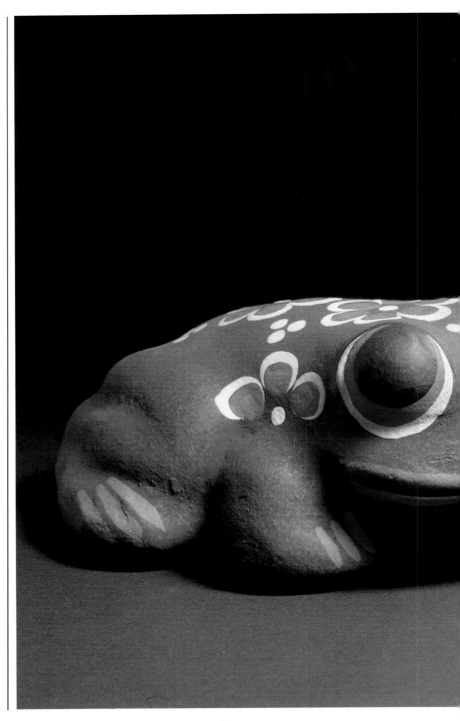

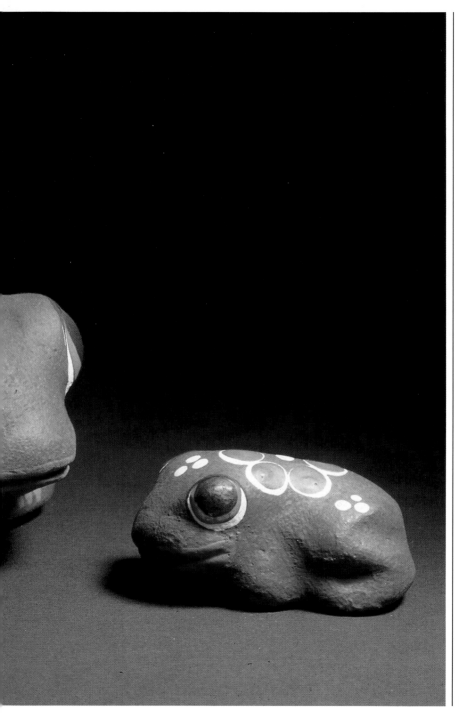

Christophe Froschauer, using the excuse that his surname contained the word *Frosch* or "frog," put a signboard outside his shop depicting a child astride a large frog.

Apart from holding out the hope of happiness in love, the frog has traditionally been hailed as the bringer of good fortune. Its likeness has thus been fashioned for this express purpose in amulets, talismans and pieces of jewellery fashioned out of precious and semi-precious stones, often engraved or

enamelled. One particular favourite is the emerald, green being the colour most strongly associated with the awakening of nature and revival of life.

Carl Fabergé, court jeweller to Tsars Alexander III and Nicholas II, and famed in all the fashionable capitals of Europe, created amusingly sensuous frogs in green jade (nephrite) with eyes set in diamonds – beautifully realized ornaments, about four inches (10 cm) high. And the frog features, too, in the Pop Art of Andy Warhol, in one of a series of animals in phosphorescent colours which also includes a panda, a monkey, an elephant, a rhinoceros, a lion and a butterfly.

In our modern age, as in centuries past, Aphrodite's little green messenger remains as bewitching and seductive as ever.

This antique bronze from Java has the face of a frog and the body of a quadruped mammal; the seductive wooden frog in bow and apron, opposite, is Italian. Preceding pages: mother and daughter from Peru.

In quest of frogs

Those of us who love frogs and everything about them will travel far and wide to enlarge our collections. We wander the shops and markets looking for objects old and new, always with an eye to a bargain but often disregarding the expense. We wear them as ornaments and as good luck tokens (laugh at us if you will, but never underestimate the magic powers of our small amphibious friends). We know that our search for frogs is far from being a waste of time.

This quest for artefacts goes hand in hand with an interest in what might be called frog lore and literature. We get enormous pleasure from discovering new rhymes and poems, coming across legends, myths and stories for the first time, lighting on allusions and references tucked away in forgotten books.

The Greek playwright Aristophanes wrote a comedy which he entitled simply *The Frogs*. And over the centuries, poets, novelists and essayists of international renown have devoted considerable space to the fascinating creature which forms the subject of our book. Some of these passages are reproduced in the following pages. These writers have been attracted to the frog for the reasons we have tried to explain, partly for its positive attributes, notably its wise, pacific and lovable character, partly for its symbolic associations with fortune and fertility, and not least for its traditional properties of magic and mystery.

With his air of scholarship and slight distraction, this pencil-holder frog seems proud of his multicoloured hairstyle.

GEORGE CATLIN, **Letters and Notes on the Manners, Customs and Conditions of the North American Indians**

Among the many letters and notes written by the author and artist George Catlin (1796-1872) in the course of his travels in search of remote tribes of American Indians, there is one text that deals with frogs. After leaving a Comanche village, tramping across the dry Texas prairie, Catlin and his friend Joe Chadwick find various fossils and minerals, and also catch sight of some strange frogs "with the horns of half and three-fourths of an inch in length, and very sharp at the points." Eager to discover other astonishing little animals, they go looking for lizards by lamplight. And in a small pond they come across a little group of frogs which seem to them even more curious than the horned species.

Several of them stopped in the middle of the pool, sitting quite "high and dry" on the surface of the water; and when we approached them nearer, or jostled them, they made a leap into the air, and coming down head foremost— went under the water and secreted themselves at the bottom. Here was a subject for Joe, in his own line! Frogs with horns, and frogs with *webbed feet*, that could hop about, and sit upon, the surface of the water! We rode around the pool and drove a number of them into it, and fearing that it would be useless to try to get one of them that evening; we rode back to the encampment, exulting very much in the curious discovery we had made for the naturalists; and by relating to some of the officers what we had seen, got excessively laughed at for our wonderful discovery! Nevertheless, Joe and I could not disbelieve what we had seen so distinctly "with our own eyes;" and we took to ourselves (or in other words, I acquiesced in Joe's taking to *himself*, as it was so peculiarly in his line) the most unequivocal satisfaction in the curious and undoubted discovery of this new variety; and we made our arrangements to ride back to the spot before "*bugle call*" in the morning; and by a thorough effort, to obtain a specimen or two of the web-footed frogs for Joe's pocket, to be by him introduced to the consideration of the knowing ones in the East. Well, our horses were saddled at an early hour, and Joe and I were soon on the spot—and he with a handkerchief at the end of a little pole,

The delightful frog from Howard Post's Dropouts *is seen here giving his throat a thorough spray — he is obviously off on a date or perhaps has a frog in his throat.*

with which he had made a sort of scoop-net, soon dipped one up as it was hopping along the surface of the water, and making unsuccessful efforts to dive through its surface. On examining its feet, we found, to our very great surprise, that we had taken a great deal of pains to entrap an old and familiar little acquaintance of our boyhood; but, somewhat like ourselves, unfortunately, from dire necessity, driven to a loathsome pool, where the water was so foul and slimy, that it could hop and dance about its surface with dry feet; and where it oftentimes found difficulty in diving through the surface to hide itself at the bottom.

I laughed a great deal at poor Joe's most cruel expense, and we amused ourselves a few minutes about this filthy and curious pool, and rode back to the encampment. We found by taking the water up in the hollow of the hand, and dipping the finger in it, and drawing it over the side, thus conducting a little of it out; it was so slimy that the whole would run over the side of the hand in a moment!

We were joked and teased a great deal about our *web-footed frogs*; and after this, poor Joe has had repeatedly to take out and exhibit his little pets in his pockets, to convince our travelling companions that *frogs sometimes actually have horns.*

THE FROG PRINCE, Traditional Fairy Tale

There are many versions of this traditional tale of the Frog Prince. They vary according to the time and culture in which they originated, but all share one essential feature: our friend the frog is always an example of common sense, wisdom and generosity.

"Princess," he said, "at last you have broken the spell. A wicked witch turned me into a frog and decreed that a frog I would remain until a Princess showed kindness to me. And you have shown true kindness, for once again I am Prince Ivan of Muscovy!"

At that moment the King walked in. He was very surprised but equally delighted at what had happened. "This is wonderful, Tania, Now you see, kindness always brings its reward!"

This soft and cuddly frog comes from the famous German Steiff factory. It is in a way a return to the past, for the first animals created by Margarethe Steiff at the beginning of the century were not made of plush but of cloth.

JOSEPH ROTH, **The Emperor's Tomb**

We are in Vienna, on the eve of the First World War. Austria and the old Hapsburg empire are still intact. As Trotta, the young hero of the novel, watches the frogs that suddenly appear, he reflects that they at least can be sure of their homeland and its future.

The land was poor, in fact, but it gave an impression of courage and freedom from care. Even the wide-stretching and uncultivable swamps seemed to me luscious and benevolent, whilst the frogs' chorus which rose from them seemed to be a hymn of praise from creatures who knew better than I did for what purpose God had created them and the swamp, their home.

BRUCE CHATWIN, **The Viceroy of Ouidah**

The Brazilian Don Francisco da Silva, future viceroy of Ouidah, kills a frog although he is well aware of the sinister consequences of the action. His forebodings are justified: setting sail for Africa to seek his fortune, he encounters only ruin..

He woke one sunrise on a patch of stony ground and, squinting sideways, was surprised to see, so far from water, a green frog crouching under the arm of a cactus. Its back was the colour of new grass, its belly mauve, and when it crawled, patches of orange and turquoise flashed from under its legs.

He poked the frog with a stick. It stiffened with fright. He watched its eyes suffuse from silver to purple. He took a stone and pounded it to a blood-streaked slime and, for a whole week, regretted what he had done.

WILLIAM SHAKESPEARE, **Macbeth**
(Act IV, scene I)

The three mysterious midnight witches, chanting spells over their hellish brew (with "toe of frog" among the ingredients), predict Macbeth's future. He will become king of Scotland, but at a price: his tragic reign will be stained by murder, madness and the terrible revenge of Malcolm, son of the slaughtered king, Duncan.

Fillet of a fenny snake,
In the cauldron boil and bake;
Eye of newt, and toe of frog,
Wool of bat, and tongue of dog,

Adder's fork, and blind-worm's sting,
Lizard's leg, and howlet's wing,
For a charm of powerful trouble,
Like a hell-broth boil and bubble.

UMBERTO ECO, **Foucault's Pendulum**

How could the magical texts of Umberto Eco not include the mysterious power of frogs? And, in fact, he actually uses them as an introduction to one of the chapters in his erudite, compelling and intriguing book, Foucault's Pendulum.

During the day you will approach the frog several times and will utter words of worship. And you will ask it to work the miracles you wish ... Meanwhile you will cut a cross on which to sacrifice it.
                                        —From a ritual of Aleister Crowley

This idyllic scene belongs to the series of Liebig animal pictures. Given away with Liebig products, these formed a huge collection, divided by subject and almost encyclopedic in coverage.

JEAN DE LA FONTAINE, **Fables**

The French scholar and poet (1621 – 1695) continued the tradition of the fable. His Fables, about 240 poems, draw on the work of Aesop and others to create a world where animals speak like men and men are described as animals. These short tales usually convey a moral.

THE FROG WHO LONGED TO BE AS BIG AS AN OX

A silly little frog
a stately Bullock spies,
and, smitten with his size,
longs to be as big.
She sucks in air. With every huff and puff
she cries, "Watch me! Am I yet big
  enough?"
– "Noo," moos the Ox – "Well, now?" –
  "Noo noo," again,

but still the Frog goes on to puff and strain.
"You're noowhere near it, you had better
  stop."
But Froggie doesn't listen – and goes POP.
  The world is full of sillies
  puffing up their bellies.
  They only have to see
  a bigger man to be
  afflicted with the swellies.

ARISTOPHANES, **The Frogs**

Staged in Athens in 405 B.C. during the feast in honour of Dionysus, The Frogs, *by Aristophanes, won first prize as the best comedy in the competition. The play, a cutting satire which engages in dispute with Euripides in particular, and angrily attacks tragedy which, "like the author, is dead," recounts the journey of Dionysus into Hades. His task is to bring back Euripides (who had died the previous year), whose worth is greater than that of the current band of new poets. While Dionysus is rowed across the River Styx by Charon, he hears a frog croaking.*

CHORUS OF FROGS.

O brood of the mere and the spring,
Gather together and sing
  From the depth of your throat
  By the side of the boat,
Co-äx, as we move in a ring;

As in Limnae we sang the divine
Nyseïan Giver of Wine,
  When the people in lots
  With their sanctified Pots
Came reeling around my shrine.

103

Donald Duck, in the guise of the bragging Leonidas W. Smiley, hero of one of Mark Twain's best stories, shows extraordinary obtuseness in trying to teach his frog friend, Daniel Webster, how to jump.

Co-äx, co-äx, co-äx,
Brekekekex co-äx.

DIONYSUS.
Don't sing anymore;
I begin to be sore!

FROGS.
Brekekekex co-äx.
Co-äx, co-äx, co-äx
Brekekekex co-äx!

DIONYSUS.
Is it nothing to you
If I'm black and blue?

FROGS.
Brekekekex co-äx!

DIONYSUS.
A plague on all of your swarming packs.
There's nothing in you except co-äx!

FROGS.
Well, and what more do you need?
Though it's none of your business indeed,
When the Muse thereanent
Is entirely content,
And horny-hoof Pan with his reed:

When Apollo is fain to admire
My voice, on account of his lyre
Which he frames with the rushes
And watery bushes—
Co-äx!—which I grow in the mire.

Co-äx, co-äx, co-äx,
Brekekekex co-äx!

DIONYSUS.
Peace, musical sisters!
I'm covered with blisters.

FROGS.
Brekekekex co-äx

Co-äx, co-äx, co-äx,
Brekekekex co-äx!
Our song we can double
Without the least trouble:
Brekekekex co-äx.

Sing we now, if ever hopping
Through the sedge and flowering
rushes;
In and out the sunshine flopping,
We have sported, rising, dropping,
With our song that nothing hushes.

Sing, if e'er in days of storm
Safe our native oozes bore us,
Staved the rain off, kept us warm,
Till we set our dance in form,
Raised our hubble-bubbling chorus:

Brekekekex co-äx, co-äx!

DIONYSUS.
Brekekekex co-äx, co-äx!
I can sing it as loud as you.

FROGS.
Sisters, that he never must do!

DIONYSUS.
Would you have me row till my shoulder
cracks?

FROGS.
Brekekekex co-äx, co-äx!

DIONYSUS.
Brekekekex co-äx, co-äx!
Groan away till you burst your backs.
It's nothing to me.

He never done nothing but...learn that frog to jump

75₵ МОНГОЛ ШУУДАН MONGOLIA

The Celebrated Jumping Frog of Calaveras County

FROGS.
Just wait till you see.

DIONYSUS.
I don't care how you scold.

FROGS.
Then all day long
We will croak you a song
As loud as our throats can hold.

Brekekekex co-äx, co-äx!!

DIONYSUS.
Brekekekex co-äx, co-äx!!
I'll see you don't outdo me in that.

FROGS.
Well, *you* shall never beat *us*—that's flat!

DIONYSUS.
I'll make you cease your song
If I shout for it all day long,
    My lungs I'll tax
    With co-äx, co-äx
—I assure you they're thoroughly strong—
Until your efforts at last relax:
Brekekekex co-äx, co-äx!!
        (*No answer from the* FROGS.)
Brekekekex co-äx, co-äx!!!
I knew in the end I should stop
    your quacks!

MARK TWAIN, **The Celebrated Jumping Frog of Calaveras County**

The famous central character of Mark Twain's story was a bullfrog. In the 1840s one Reverend Leonidas W. Smiley turned up in the county of Calaveras. A schemer and gambler, he would bet on anything … even on jumping frogs.

He ketched a frog one day, and took him home, and said he cal'lated to educate him; and so he never done nothing for three months but set in his back yard and learn that frog to jump. And you bet you he *did* learn him, too. He'd give him a little pinch behind, and the next minute you'd see that frog whirling in the air like a doughnut –

105

The Celebrated Jumping Frog of Calaveras County

...ot the frog out and filled him full of quail shot.

see him turn one summerset, or maybe a couple, if he got a good start, and come down flat-footed and all right, like a cat. He got him up so in the matter of ketching flies, and kep' him in practice so constant, that he'd nail a fly every time as fur as he could see him. Smiley said all a frog wanted was education, and he could do 'most anything – and I believe him. Why, I've seen him set Dan'l Webster down her on this floor – Dan'l Webster was the name of the frog – and sing out, 'Flies, Dan'l, flies!' and quicker 'n you could wink he'd spring straight up and snake a fly off 'n the counter there, and flop down on the floor ag'in as solid as a gob of mud and fall to scratching the side of his head with his hind foot as indifferent as if he hadn't no idea he'd been doin' any more'n any frog might do. You never see a frog so modest and straightfor'ard as he was, for all he was so gifted. And when it came to fair and square jumping on a dead level, he could get over more ground at one straddle than any animal of his breed you ever see. Jumping on a dead level was his strong suit, you understand, and when it came to that, Smiley would ante up money on him as long as he had a red. Smiley was monstrous proud of his frog, and well he might be, for fellers that had traveled and been everywheres all said he laid over any frog that ever *they* see.

Here the naughty cousin Gus plays the part of Smiley's rival, who is pouring quail shot down the throat of the jumping frog in order to win the bet, just as in Mark Twain's story. Below: the Dropouts frog again, this time in pursuit of an unlucky, innocent butterfly.

PUBLIUS OVIDUS NASO, **Metamorphoses**

In his Metaporphoses, *Ovid tells the story of Latona, daughter of the Titan Coeus. Wooed and made pregnant by Zeus, Latona is forced to wander through the lands of the Aegean in search of a safe place to give birth, and eventually arrives at Delos. But she even has to flee this island, persecuted by Juno, bent on revenge. Reaching Lycia, exhausted by her long journey and assailed by heat and thirst, she sees a lake in the distance and comes near to drink. As she approaches, some peasants bar her way and threaten her.*

Nor is this enough. They likewise muddy the lake itself *with* their feet and hands; and they raise the soft mud from the very bottom of the water, by spitefully jumping to and fro. Resentment removes her thirst. For now no longer does the daughter of Caeus supplicate the unworthy *wretches*, nor does she any longer endure to utter words below *the majesty of* a Goddess; and raising her hands to heaven, she says, 'For ever may you live in that pool.' The wish of the Goddess comes to pass. They delight to go beneath the water, and sometimes to plunge the whole of their limbs in the deep pool; now to raise their heads, and now to swim on the top of the water; often to sit on the bank of the pool, *and* often to leap back again into the cold stream. And even now do they exercise their offensive tongues in strife: and banishing *all* shame, although they are beneath the water, *still* beneath the water, do they try to keep up their abuse. Their voice, too, is now hoarse, and their bloated necks swell out; and their very abuse dilates their extended jaws. Their backs are united to their heads; their necks seem as though cut off; their backbone is green; their belly, the greatest part of their body, is white; and, *as* new-made frogs, they leap about in the muddy stream.

This gold and diamond frog brooch is a fine example of modern jewellery: the jacket lapel is a far cry from the lily pad.

Idioms and proverbs

A short glossary of frogs in four languages

English

frog *n.* (from Old English, *frogga*) tailless amphibious animal || fastening of military cloak || attachment for carrying sword || horny substance on sole of a horse's foot || (*fig.*) *frog in one's throat,* hoarse.

frogman *n.* underwater divers for special tasks, salvage, demolition, exploration, etc.

frogmarch *n.* method of carrying a prisoner face downwards by four persons holding arms and legs || *v.t.* to carry a prisoner in this way.

frog sticker *n.* American slang for a knife, usually carried as a weapon.

toad *n.*(from Old English *tadige*) froglike amphibious animal || (*fig.*) disgusting, unpleasant individual.

toadeater *n. (rare)* fawning, sycophantic person.

toad–in–the–hole *n.* a term used in British cookery for a dish made of sausages baked in batter.

toady *n.* obsequious sycophant || *v.i.* to fawn, to be a toady.

toadyism *n.* servile flattery, sycophancy.

French

grenouille *n.f.*(from vulg. Lat. *ranucola*) frog || *homme-grenouille*, frogman ||

109

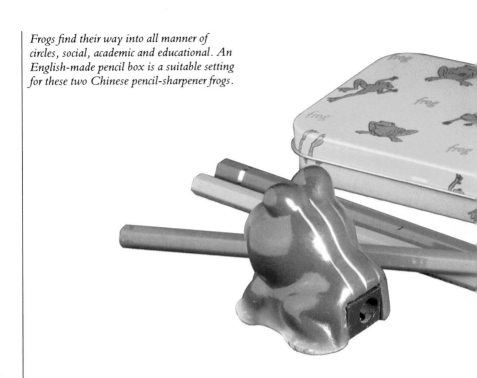

Frogs find their way into all manner of circles, social, academic and educational. An English-made pencil box is a suitable setting for these two Chinese pencil-sharpener frogs.

(*fig.*) *elle est gonflée comme la grenouille de la fable*, she is as conceited as the frog in the fable, with reference to Aesop || *manger la grenouille, faire sauter la grenouille*, make off with the cash, get away with the money.

crapaud *n.m.* (from hypothetical Germanic *Krappa*) toad || (*fig.*) ugly or rude person.

crapoussin *n.m.* (*fig.*) a lively child, kid; (*lit.*) a dwarf, freak.

Italian

rana *n.f.* (from vulg. Lat. *rana*) frog || (*fig.*) an ugly deformed person || (*military jargon*) recruit newly arrived at the barracks || (*fig.*) *gonfio come una rana*, puffed-up, arrogant, boastful || *camminare come una rana*, to walk with a leap in the step || *avere le gambe come una rana*, to have bandy legs || *uomini-rana*, underwater divers carrying out special duties || *nuoto a rana*, breaststroke || *andar per rane*, popular way of saying to waste time || *vai a rane, vai a ranare*, popular Milanese ways of telling someone to get lost.

rospo *n.m.* (from vulg. Lat. *broscus* and class. Lat. *ruspari*) toad || (*fig.*) contemptuous expression to describe a person, who because of his or her ugliness, inspires repulsion || bad-tempered, unsociable person || *ingoiare il rospo*, to

accept reluctantly a disagreeable fact or situation || *sputare il rospo*, to get something off one's chest.

German

Frosch *n.m.* (-(e)s. Frösche) (from Germanic *frosk*) frog || *(fig.) sei kein Frosch!*, don't be a coward, don't make a fuss || *sich wie ein Frosch aufblasen*, to puff oneself up, give oneself airs || *einen Frosch im Hals haben*, to be hoarse || *Frösche in den Bauch kriegen*, to have a rumbling stomach from drinking too much || *Froschbauch*, flabby, protruding stomach || *Froschblut haben*, to be cold-blooded, unemotional || *daliegen wie ein geprellter Frosch*, lie exhausted || *dasitzen wie der Frosch auf der Gießkanne*, sit wrapped in thought.

Kröte *n.f.* (from Old Germanic *Krota* or *Kreta*) toad || *(fig.) so eine freche Kröte!*, what a cheeky child || *meine letzten Kröten*, my last few coins (popular expression, probably arising from the image of a tortoise – *Schildkröte* – on old Greek coins).

Acknowledgements

This book would not have been possible without the contributions of many frog enthusiats and their collections. The authors would like to thank the owners of the objects photographed and the following:
Marco Campogiani (antique dealer, Milan), Giorgio Cavallari, Rosi Comensoli and Gianfranco Rossi (Ethno Arte, Milan), Marina and Nino De Col (Gog & Magog, Milan), Francesca Del Signore (as frog on p. 62), Maurizio Epifani (L'oro dei farlocchi, Milan), Mariangela Fardella, Luigi Sapino (Galleria Mirabilia, Turin).

The publisher thanks Gruppo Mantero for allowing the reproduction of the Interseta design on the cover.

Quote on p. 100 from *The Emperor's Tomb* by Joseph Roth, first published in 1984 by The Overlook Press. Lewis Hollow Road, Woodstock, New York $15.95.

Picture sources

The frogs illustrated in this book belong to the following collections:
Marica and Antonio Anderlini (pp. 20-21, 35);
Nicol Balzani (pp. 8-9, 18, 19, 23, 25, 27, 29, 47, 57, 59, 63, 68-69, 84, 87, 92-93, 94);
Carla Cherubini (cover, pp. 2, 10, 13, 17, 30, 32-33, 36, 37, 39, 44, 46, 48-49, 51, 53, 56, 66, 67, 73, 76, 83, 85, 91, 95, 108);
Marina and Nino De Col (pp. 7, 101);
Anna Giorgetti (p. 12);
Grazia Lissi (p. 90);
Iro Novak (pp. 45, 70, 75, 86, 110-111);
Marina Robbiani (pp. 14, 28, 50, 55, 61, 62, 64-65, 71, 78, 80, 81, 88-89, 96);
Paolo Romoli (pp. 11, 14, 22, 24, 31, 40, 41, 42, 43, 54, 60, 74, 79, 102, 105, 106);

All photographs by Giorgio Coppin in collaboration with Anna Giorgetti, Marco Melloni and Sara Sfligiotti.